Raindrops on My Window

Dr. Omkar Bhatkar

Ukiyoto Publishing

All global publishing rights are held by

Ukiyoto Publishing

Published in 2023

Content Copyright © Dr. Omkar Bhatkar

Cover Photograph by Krutika Shinde

ISBN 9789359203058

All rights reserved.

No part of this publication may be reproduced, transmitted, or stored in a retrieval system, in any form by any means, electronic, mechanical, photocopying, recording or otherwise, without the prior permission of the publisher.

The moral rights of the author have been asserted.

This is a work of fiction. Names, characters, businesses, places, events, locales, and incidents are either the products of the author's imagination or used in a fictitious manner. Any resemblance to actual persons, living or dead, or actual events is purely coincidental.

This book is sold subject to the condition that it shall not by way of trade or otherwise, be lent, resold, hired out or otherwise circulated, without the publisher's prior consent, in any form of binding or cover other than that in which it is published.

*Dedicated to
Mom and Dad*

*Pedro Magalhães
Pratibha Joshi
Sunil Noronha
Ignasi Vendrell
Mark Aumoine
Nishtha Juneja*

Contents

Characters	1
Scene I: Feelings	3
Scene II: Roles- A Scene From The Past	14
Scene III: Attempts To Rework	16
Scene IV: The Cafe	27
About the Author	*34*

Characters

Smita

Smita spent most of her life balancing her work and home. Her work as a librarian is her only solace that allows her an escape from her home. She is a clear, practical, and emotional woman. She isn't exactly concerned with societal pressure and makes her own decision. She is independent, well-read, and intelligent. Simple joys of life like the rain make her happy. Her life mainly revolves around her home, children, and husband. Her solace is her books and the joys of drinking hot cups of tea in the rain.

Nishikant

Nishikant is a workaholic. He dedicates most of his time to his business affairs. But also fulfills his responsibilities as father and husband. With his economic support he brings comfort to the family but in the process has lost touch with Smita whom he loves very much. Smita takes care of the children and familial responsibilities and Nishikant admires her for the same. But in performing the societal roles assigned to them they gradually lose the connection with each other. He has always been a stereotypical man of the house and is not accustomed to showing his inner turmoil. A lot is left unsaid.

Both of them have three grown-up children. Smita and Nishikant have been married together for about 23 years. In spite of being together, there is an emptiness that eventually takes the form of boredom.

The play premiered in Mumbai at St. Andrew's Centre for Philosophy and Performing Arts in August 2022, Directed by Dr. Omkar Bhatkar, Nishikant was played by Prasant Nalaskar and Smita was played by Rekha Shetty.

Scene I: Feelings

In The living room of an upper-middle-class family and a lonely woman (Smita) in the house at about 11 in the morning who has just finished her morning chores, is reading a poetry book interrupted by a phone ring. The house is filled with the morning rain pouring from all open windows and white sheer curtains moving with the breeze.

(Ye re ghana...♪ could be played from the album *Aawaz Chandnyache* sung by Asha Bhosle)

The Phone Rings

Smita :

Yes, I am. How are you? And how is Sarah?

Smita :

Ofcourse, I will come for Sarah's convocation, not a question to ask.

Smita :

Yes, Nishi asked me too yesterday. But I wasn't sure if you would be okay with it, so I did not say anything.

Smita :

Priya, Nishikant, and I have no qualms between us. Don't worry about it. I think you're overthinking our decision to separate, it's not that aggressive or ugly.

You anyway will be coming home today, right?

Smita :

Alright! Let's peacefully talk then.

Nishikant enters the stage conversing on the phone in Marathi talking incoherently with someone else

Light Fades

The light slowly changes to warm yellow from white and Smita addresses the audience then slowly moves to do odd cleaning jobs in the house while saying her lines throughout the scene.

Smita (to herself) :

Why does everyone think that I'm unhappy? How do they feel that we both can't cope? Why is everyone behaving like this? When we made this decision all the close and distant family and neighbours came to talk to us, as if something was wrong with what we were doing. They even asked us to go for counseling. Some of them said it would separate this unit called family. One of them actually said maybe it's because the biological clock is ticking, and he must be having no interest in me. Some of them seemed to know better than us and simply said 'There is nothing wrong, just that both of us are behaving childlike and stupid'.

Another profile spot on Nishkant dressed in his formal attire, sitting at his desk which is in the house but has the look of an office desk

Nishikant (to himself) :

My son, Raghuvendra, doubted or more or less questioned me if I had someone else in my life. I still don't know if he was so caring about his mother, that he actually kept an eye on me and started following me to the places I frequented.

What surprised me is that he read my WhatsApp messages,

He thought I didn't figure it out. I did and I just pretended that everything was alright. Is it really important to have someone in life as a cause in order to leave another person? I won't deny that I had someone else in my life. But this wasn't at the time when I decided to separate from Smita.

No one could match what Smita was and is in my life today. She is the dawn of my life and maybe that's the problem. One can't remain awake forever, one also needs the darkness of the night........

Smita (to herself) :

We both think we know the reasons but actually, we both know that there are no reasons, and maybe that's reason enough.

Nishikant had asked me for divorce after 23 years of marriage. But it was only the day I was reading an article by an author whose name I've forgotten by now which propelled me to act upon what he had asked three years back.

I shouldn't have read that article whose name I don't remember. He was a Danish philosopher, his writing left me with sleepless nights with his idea that 'it's better to be lost in passion than to lose passion.

Nishikant (to himself) :

She has always lived a secure life with me. I'm surprised she took this risk to say yes. But everything is now repetitive, each day exactly like the previous one.

And passion? Well, I love my wife. It's not that I don't love her but then there is nothing to look forward to. I can't keep on going like this…….. there is a sense of meaninglessness lingering in this marriage now.

Smita (to herself) :

Every morning, when I open my eyes to the so-called 'new day', I feel like closing them again, staying in bed, and not getting up. Listen to the relentless rain that douses the sound of everything else. I don't feel like getting freshened up or venturing into the kitchen. But I can't do that. Can I?

Since I married Nishikant the hands of the clock became slower and slower until they just stopped. Life paused in eternal repetitiveness.

Nishikant (to himself) :

I wonder if the battery of the clock is over. But we tried changing the battery by recharging it. We went on holiday, just both of us. We even read together, and attended concerts together. We started spending a lot of time together, yes it worked for some time. Last year we even went to Ladakh though she was insistent that we should go to Cherrapunji. I didn't understand what we would do in Cherrapunji and that also in November.

Smita (to herself) :

It rains there even in November, he didn't even know that.

Nishikant (to himself) :

God knows where she read about this oro…

Smita (to herself) :

Orographic Rain, the monsoon clouds fly unhindered over the plains of Bangladesh for long distances like a magical carpet floating in the blue sky. Thereafter, they hit the velvet green Khasi Hills, The geography of the hills with many deep valley channels encompassing the low-flying moisture-laden clouds from a wide area converges over Cherrapunji. This extreme amount of rainfall is perhaps the best-known feature of orographic rain in northeastern India. But he didn't even bother to know more.

All he knows is that he doesn't want to go to Cherrapunji.

Nishikant (to himself) :

I don't know which touristy books she reads in her library. And touristy books should write about the snow of the Himalayas and not the landscape of Cherrapunji. I wonder if she read it in some geography book.

Smita (to herself) :

We ended up going to Himachal.

Nishikant (to himself) :

But when we were back at home we resumed our same old mundane life. || There were times when I desired her and she would be wrapped in putting Mana to sleep.

Smita (to herself) :

As much as I longed to wrap myself in his arms. There were nights when I was so tired that I just fell asleep in the kid's room. || Love was slowly fading. As the hands of the clock were slowing down, there came a time when time just stopped. It was then I read the article.

What's wrong with routine and boredom?

Nishikant (to himself) :

Boredom, the state of being weary and restless through lack of interest.

Smita and Nishikant (to themselves) :

Yes, we both had lost interest in each other, in this marriage which was nothing else but a routine.

Nishikant (to himself) :

What if she leaves me one day?

The first thing I did was try to answer all my questions. And the more questions I answered, the more questions appeared. Is she in love with someone else? We don't even make love as often as we used to, Is she already with someone else?

Smita (to herself) :

Does he think I've found someone else because I haven't shown much interest in sex for the last three years? To have no interest in sex could have myriad reasons than just being with someone else.

We never have jealous spats, and I used to think that was great, but after one morning. I began to suspect that perhaps our lack of jealousy meant indifference.

After spending some time at the library, I used to come home and enter the enchanted realm of my domestic world, everything would seem marvelous for a few hours until everyone went to bed. Then, slowly the nightmare would begin.......

Nishikant (to himself) :

I couldn't sleep those nights. When night used to fall and Smita was deep asleep, I would tiptoe to the balcony, light my cigarette, and gaze at the stars in the sky. It used to be those fragile moments of realization when I would question myself if love and marriage were the same things. Or is everything beautiful and magical when it's new and fresh? Once the chase is over and we have that beauty in our hands then do we lose its essence? Isn't so that all novelties quickly become habits.

And the dreadful feeling that I'm wasting the best years of my life in a pattern that will be repeated over and over until I die like a falling star, burning in my own glory.

Smita (to herself) :

I tried to distract myself from these thoughts. I started reading women's fashion magazines at the library; I even started solving the newspaper crosswords every day. At times, I would be shopping at the supermarket unnecessarily and feeding the family with different dishes. I even thought of volunteering at the Old Age home nearby, so as to seek consolation in other people's suffering.

Nishikant (to himself) :

I open the newspaper and read it from start to end. I see endless reports about accidents, people made homeless by the Tsunami, migration crisis. The pandemic that killed an entire generation of old people in Spain.

The rising dissent and mob lynching, the rising unemployment, and the spread of hate crime.

Smita (to herself) :

I changed channels. I subscribed to Netflix and I saw movies day and night. For a couple of hours, I used to forget everything. At night, I used to be terrified that my husband would wake up and ask: 'What's wrong Smit? And what else could I say but just that nothing, everything is fine.

One night I saw a film. I don't remember its title now that after the divorce a single woman goes on a trip to Europe and ends up buying a villa in ruins there and decides to make it a new home and never come back.

It was then I realized that I was a woman torn between the terror that everything might change and the equal terror that everything might carry on exactly the same for the rest of my days.

Nishikant (to himself) :

The marriage seemed pointless now. A journey should have a purpose; our marriage has ceased its purpose and I see no point in taking it anywhere. It's not that Smit has some faults, but it's just that I don't see any faults. Marriage after twenty-three years has just become a routine, it's nothing more than a habit.

Keeping the same fire burning after twenty-three years of marriage seems a complete impossibility to me. And each time I pretend in front of her that everything is alright, I die a little inside.

Smita (to herself) :

There were also times when I felt that my life made perfect sense, that this is the role of a partner to complete the incompleteness.

'The children feel that their mother is so full of joy, their father is there when needed and the whole house symbolizes perfection. Each one doing their part efficiently and therefore the family, and the house seemed perfect.

We probably were inspiring to others or envied by our friends and extended family. I really don't know, but we were a family that stayed together happily.

And then suddenly for no reason I would get into the shower and burst into tears. I can cry there because no one can hear my sobs or ask me that question I hate the most "Are you alright?"

Nishikant (to himself) :

Sometimes, when I've asked her anything. She would just get up slowly as if she didn't hear me, walk to the window, and keep looking at the hazy outlines of trees in the window. She just doesn't speak at times. I wonder if it's the rain or it's something else.

Smita (to herself) :

Such is the nature of one's soul in the monsoon season which makes us look into the intricacies of our souls which wouldn't be possible in other seasons like the monsoon does. Sometimes the outpouring is so powerful that it shuts all the noises and all you can hear is rain. That is when you listen to yourself.

Nishikant (to himself) :

It's difficult to understand her now. I wonder when she became so unpredictable!

Smita (to herself) :

It's silly for me now to blame Kierkegaard or the film that I saw. The article only made me think about what was always inside me, just that I never acknowledged it.

Nishikant (to himself):

I believe that some people spend years allowing the pressure to build up inside them without even noticing, and then one day some tiny incident triggers a crisis.

Smita and Nishikant (together):

'I've had enough, I don't want this anymore

Smita *(to herself)* :

Women like me only think and don't act upon our thoughts. I know that

I will repress my feelings until cancer starts eating me up inside.

Blackout

(Paus datlela ♪ can be played from the album *Gaarva* by Milind Ingle)

Scene II: Roles- A Scene From The Past

Nishikant :

It's 6-30 am. I think you should go and get Mana up.

Smita :

Why don't we swap roles for once? You go to the kitchen and I water the plants.

Nishikant :

Is that a challenge?

Smita :

No, it isn't a challenge. I just want to change things around a bit.

Smita :

After watering the plants, I took a shower and what I saw was the table perfectly set with fruits, bread, butter, poha. It is indeed a great breakfast.

Nishi, we need to have a talk tonight.

Nishikant :

Let's go somewhere to dine then.

Smita :

Somewhere, without music blaring in our ears and somewhere quiet where people aren't talking at the top of their voices. Somewhere peaceful! Bandra has become a very noisy place to eat or dine.

Lights gradually Fade out

(Chhaya Ghanaichhe Bone Bone ♪ can be played written by Rabindranath Tagore and sung by Hemant Kumar)

Scene III: Attempts To Rework

They both eating at a white round table in the center of the stage, with only one spotlight on them

Nishikant (to himself) :

We eat in silence. The waiter has already been to our table twice to see if we've finished, but we haven't even touched our plates. I can imagine what she is thinking while she is gulping the wine down her throat. She is thinking of me as to how to make me understand her state, her apathy.

Smita (to herself) :

I can imagine what he is thinking while he is gulping the wine down his throat. How can I help Smit? What can I do to make her happy?

Nothing, nothing more than he's doing already. I would dislike it if he arrived home bearing some new dress and a bouquet of flowers.

Nishikant (to himself) :

I can easily get a new saree for her but I'm aware that she would not like it.

But what exactly is missing from our life?

Smita (to herself) :

Marriage has become a habit, a routine. Am I echoing Nishi's words? All that we do is take care of responsibilities. When children were young, we took intrinsic care of them. As they grew, they needed more attention. We spent more time with our children than we did with ourselves. However, I believe it was the need of the hour. Schooling, College, and finally today all three of them are in different directions. It's only my youngest daughter who visits us often and then there is little life in the house. Otherwise, the house is a walk in the cemetery. We discuss Kanta's salary, banking details, newspaper bills, electricity bills, grocery bills, medicines, and the never-ending repairs.

Nishikant (to himself) :

Yes, how can we forget the repairs? It all started when we bought a new Projector and it required a blank empty wall. So we got the wall repainted white but then the other three walls were dull, so we also painted them. The ceiling color was odd, so we chose a color to complement the walls and finally, the chandelier was abrupting the way so we got it removed but there was no good yellow night for evenings and finally we got a new standing lamp. Gradually, the refurbishment spread to the whole house.

Smita (to herself) :

I hope the same doesn't happen to my life. I hope that the small things won't lead to great transformations.

Nishikant gets up while reciting the following line and moves around the area of his office desk

Nishikant (to himself):

I've made a list of things to do after reading a little here and there.

Smita gets up while reciting the following line and moves around the area of her reading table

Smita (to herself):

I too have my own list of things to do to protect myself from falling back into a black hole.

(long pause)

Smita (to audience):

I prefer to cook. Cooking helps me to concentrate. It involves all the five senses and I feel joyful when I feed my family.

Nishikant (to audience):

Every time I feel angry about something, I try not to react but just keep quiet. Often, just go to the washroom and put water on my face. Water washes the dirt from the mind.

Smita (to audience):

I drink a lot of cold water. Water invigorates me.

Nishikant (to audience):

I spend hours gazing at the night sky.

Smita (to audience) :

I spend hours gazing at the sun sinking in the sea.

Nishikant (to audience) :

I try to wear glasses every day to hide my sleepless eyes.

Smita (to audience) :

I smile, even if I feel like crying. It's difficult but I try hard. Probably, I'm good at it as no one has noticed my pain.

Nishikant (to audience) :

I'm on tindr, I try spending time there chatting with people online but I've no inclination to meet anyone. Just a past time.

Smita (to audience) :

I visit my past through pictures and some letters that I hide deep in my soul.

Nishikant (to audience) :

I play Candy Crush to distract me.

Smita (to audience) :

I keep on streaming films online to distract me.

Nishikant (to audience) :

I wish monsoon never arrives

Nishikant (to audience) :

Monsoon is my only solace and it seems I live the year waiting for this one season.

(long pause)

(Sounds of thunder and rain can be used here, the scene transits into a scene from the past)

Smita (to herself):

How can I forget that rainy evening! I was drenched in rain walking over my footpath near the Mayor's Bungalow. I crossed the road when the signal was still green and as I stepped on the footpath of Barista. I saw through the foggy window Nishikant sipping coffee with Aratrika. I could look at him through that window even if it was hazy, raindrops on the window and both of them wrapped in the warmth of yellow light. I dialed his number from my phone, but he didn't answer.

I waited.

I was about to call again

and

He texted me saying that …..

Nishikant (to himself):

I'm in a meeting, I shall call you later.

Smita (to herself):

Nishikant is sitting with Aratrika, sipping coffee. If someone had told me I might have not believed it to be true. But here he was right in front of my eyes.

Finally, I have a solid reason to be jealous about something.

Manish had been calling me for so many days to catch up over a coffee, but I always made some excuses. I didn't want to meet a college friend, now. I guess we both were attracted to each other, but we didn't let that spark turn into fire. Later, we lost touch.

A few months ago, he got in touch. But I didn't make time. This time I thought, let me also dive into an adventure. After all our marriage has just become a habit.

Nishikant (to himself) :

And what if it had been my wife who'd found a long-lost friend or even love? How would I have reacted?

I would have said that life is unfair, that I'm worthless, and I'm getting old.

I would have screamed bloody whore.

I would have envied her and smoked endlessly and gazed at the night sky, from jealousy.

I would have asked her to leave, shutting the door behind me. Our children are anyway not around.

Smita (to herself) :

Boredom can make us do crazy things. And going after a dream has its price. Manish wasn't a dream but an adventure for sure.

And I picked up Manish's call, which I had ignored for so long. I needed a friend, a company, or maybe love. Someone who could make me smile again, and take me on new adventures. Someone who could make me laugh, and hold my hands to know that I'm not alone.

I did this because I felt alone, I did this because I thought our marriage was a routine. I did this because I needed a break from mundaneness. I didn't do it only because I saw him with Aratrika that evening, but yes it did help me to make a decision that I had postponed so far.

I don't want to long back in life one day and ask myself what if I had opened that door to Manish? I don't want to be caught up in a conundrum of decisions not made. I don't want to regret it even if it meant putting all the very little left on stake. The children were grown up and I had done my duties as a mother. I didn't fail as a wife either but as myself, did I fail to myself? It's time I do something for my own happiness even if it means being selfish. Our whole life we spend in giving ourselves to others, let me give it to myself.

(Chhaya Ghanaichhe Bone Bone contd…♪)

Nishikant (to himself) :

With time Smita lost all the remaining passion which had only stayed in last three years. Love finally is a habit. She slowly gave up taking care of things at home, because she thought:

Smita (to herself) :

If I can balance the outside world of work and the inside world of home then definitely he can.

Nishikant (to himself) :

Unfortunately, my mother had not raised me to take care of homely concerns. But slowly I had to take care of everything from keeping the house clean to laundry, to paying bills of all kinds. From taking care of the needs of children abroad to what Kanta needed in the kitchen, I did it.

I was fighting the domestic battles alone. Smit had given up over taking care of anything. I could have screamed and shouted. But would that help? That would just add to nothing else but a fight and probably a separation. And was it separation that I needed?

Smita (to herself) :

I started going out often. I spent much more time in the library followed by meeting Manish almost every day. But slowly I also realised that it didn't make such a big difference. I wasn't paying much attention to home and my husband. I occasionally spoke to my children. I had shrugged away most responsibilities that tied me at home. I was spending time with a man who longed for my company. I was free, but not 'happy'. Isn't this all that I wanted? And if it is I wonder why I wasn't happy?

Nishikant (to himself) :

Gradually, I was beginning to like domestic chores. I felt Smita's absence from the home. Something had to be done about both of us. We at 45 were moving away from each other, and the reason was unreasonable. I'm well aware I'm not in love with Aratrika or for that sake anyone else but Smit. I still long for her touch, I still yearn to have my breakfast with her. I still yearn to see her happy. I yearn for us to be like before.

Smita (to herself) :

Can things be like before? A question that haunts me every day. Can we ever be like before, two different souls entwined in one beautiful relationship; completing the incomplete part of each other?

But why should things be like before?

Am I still 30 years old?

Do we have no children?

Are we still in college watching a film at Roxy?

Of course, we are not. We are not the same people we were when we were 30. Nishikant has changed, I'm changed and Change is inevitable. How could we still be the same person over a span of 30 years?

If we ourselves are not the same, how can our marriage- our relationships remain just like before?

Nishikant (to himself) :

If our relationship isn't like before, and if it's going to become worse with time then it's time to stop here. It's time to stop before it rots. Let's move out of each other's lives. Let's give each other space. Why should we be burdened with boredom? Do we want to reach a stage where we kill our own marriage and then say 'Maybe it wasn't worth it'? Before we reach there, let's pause here and walk our individual paths. And if that way Smit will be happy, then I shall be happy too.

Smita (to herself) :

Maybe I want space but with Nishikant it's not that he doesn't give me my space. The moment he realizes that I want my own time he moves out of it without any questions.

Is separation the only way to happiness? But if it is then did it take us 23 years for us to realize that we are not meant for each other? And what is the guarantee that even with Manish this state won't arrive in the next 3 years? Just yesterday, again I had an argument with Manish. It's been a week in his company but I can't say I'm very happy, it's almost the same feeling that I had with Nishikant in our earlier days, but it all changed with time. Will it change with Manish too and it will be nothing else but the same boredom with another man, do I need to go down the same journey again to find the same thing?

Am I even looking for love with him?

Because if it's love then none has loved me like Nishi! And if I know that then why am I even thinking of separation? I'm sure Nishikant has noticed the way I spend time with Manish but he has never questioned me. Does he trust me that much?

I still don't know if it's love for Manish or the desire to be with him so that I could be the younger version of myself in his company. Do I long for Manish or I want to relive my younger days?

Am I lost in this adventure that I've taken?

Nishikant (to himself) :

I was lost.

Smita (to herself) :

He was lost and I was lost.

Nishikant- Smita (together) :

If we both are lost then we will just drive each other crazy, it's better to separate and leave it at a beautiful point.

(Raha Dekhe… ♪ can be played in the film Raincoat by Shubha Mudgal and Debojyoti Mishra)

Gradually the lights fade out

Scene IV: The Cafe

(After three years of divorce, Smita and Nishikant decide to meet each other. The Meeting takes place at the same restaurant where they dined earlier, in the center of the stage)

Nishikant :

It's been three years.

Smita :

It's been three years,

Nishikant :

How are you spending your time?

Smita :

The day passes somehow, at evenings I try to catch up with school or college time friends, and Manish joins when he can.

I invent things to kill time, I have too much of it on my hand here.

(Both of them talk incoherently, in disjointed - incomplete sentences)

Smita :

How do you pass your time?

Nishikant :

There should be time Smita, It's been three years since I've taken care of the home.

It was then I realized that I was never a part of the household, of everything that you did on your own. You never complained about it. You managed everything without me......

What must you be feeling?

Don't you have any resentment?

Smita :

Resentments don't help in conjugal life. If I had started to feel disappointed about every small thing, then I guess the marriage cart wouldn't have been pulled for twenty-three years then…..

Nishikant :

I want to save our marriage; I want to see both of us happy together. I love you. I would endure anything, absolutely anything to have you by my side. And if you still wish to leave me someday, then I can't stop you from that. So if that day comes, you are free to leave and seek your happiness. But please let's start all over again from a blank slate. In the last three years, I've realized that there is nothing more important for me than both of us. I have walked this journey with you for twenty-three years. I have seen the rising sun with you and I would also like to see the sun set of life with you.

(long pause)

I'm not afraid of loneliness. These three years made me see a different Diwali, a different Christmas, and even a different monsoon season, it's a different house in spite of everything being the same yet nothing like what I had with you.

I may not have been the best husband in the world, because I hardly ever showed my feelings. I'm sorry for going away from you and leaving you behind. I will come to Cherrapunji to see your oro....

Orographic rains *(puts hand in his phone and checks the word)*

Perhaps, you might ask me why I'm back again. Let's not jump into any long-term decisions. Let us not seek answers that we already know and don't want to accept.

If we don't live together, can we go out together for a few days, just the both of us, wherever you say, We can go to New Zealand, Maldives or even Tuscany as you always wanted to go there.

Smita :

You're changed and still the same. Not the summer of Tuscany but the monsoon of Konkan. Let's go to our ancestral home in Ratnagiri. We can sit throughout the day listening to the rain falling on the clay tiles singing a song of the rain and gazing at the raindrops on my (our) window.

Lights fade slowly and music

(Konkanchi Chedva can be played from the album *Maazhi Gaani* by Vaishali Samant and Avadhoot Gupte…♪)

Curtain

"When you love each other, you have to be ready for anything. Because love is like a kaleidoscope, the kind we used to play with when we were kids. It's in constant movement and never repeats itself. If you don't understand this, you're condemned to suffer from something that really only exists to make us happy".

Writer - Director Note

Raindrops on My Window is written and directed for stage as a simple story with deep emotional statements and questions that set the existential clock ticking. Both the characters in the play aren't bitter about each other but have reached a stage in life where they are unable to help a relationship falling apart or a relationship not able to stay together. The story is concerned with everyday reality and helplessness laced with an ever-increasing boredom of togetherness. Raindrops on My Window is an attempt to sit and talk to oneself observing the passage of time and the ever-changing self. Therefore, most often the characters face the audience and talk to themselves with occasional scenes where they actually talk to each other. The conversation with themselves facing the audience is actually a conversation with the audience who too would be grappling with the same questions or have been in the same boat. The writing is subtle and therefore the play demands subtle direction, acting, set, and light design. The story may come across as repetitive but that's the nature of our life where often the same things repeat themselves in myriad similar ways. The songs mentioned in the play are suggestive, the Director is free to choose music of their choice or even use live music to accompany the play.

For public performances and staging of the play kindly get in touch on metamorphosistheatreinc@gmail.com

Critics Note

Two loving souls living under the same roof suffer the loss of not only the novelty but the meaning of life as they go through the years of routine, languishing in ever-increasing misery and loneliness, looking for alternatives. It cannot be said that this midlife crisis is only an urban upper-middle-class reality but also a visceral phenomenon across societies of different kinds and its tragedy only becomes darker. Omkar Bhatkar's literature explores the purposelessness of life, the boredom that overwhelms relationships, and the basic human loneliness through flowing repetitive soliloquies. In a boring routine, seemingly pointless moments can also act as a ticking time bomb. Indecisive milestones become an endless pattern. Through myriad micro-spaces, the play raises many fundamental questions about love and togetherness.

'Raindrops on My Window' is a must-have theater experience. Nishikant and Smita portrayed by Prashant Nalskar and Rekha Shetty are memorable because they wanted to project a crumbling romantic life without any aggressive confrontational input. The ending is a light pleasant shock conveyed in the most meaningful way possible. Geographies of Faraway Cherrapunji and the Konkan shore are recurring poetic motifs in the play that render an interior depth to the character's state of being.

-Bharti Birje Diggikar
Poet, Translator

About the Author

Dr. Omkar Bhatkar

Dr. Omkar Bhatkar is a Sociologist with a doctoral thesis concerned with Proxemics and Social Ecology. He has been a visiting professor for a decade now teaching Film Theory, Culture Studies, and Gender Studies. He has also served as a faculty for the London School of Economics International Programmes in Sociology. He is the Co-Founder and Head of 'St. Andrew's Centre for Philosophy and Performing Arts, Mumbai. Dr. Omkar Bhatkar runs his own theatre group known as Metamorphosis Theatre and Films. His works largely focus on Poetry in Motion, Existentialist Themes, and Contemporary French Plays in Translation. Dr. Bhatkar's play 'Blue Storm' was selected at the Asia Playwrights Theatre Festival 2021 held in South Korea. Though he is grounded in theatre, he also explores the world of films as an independent filmmaker making feature-length narrative films and documentaries. He is a tormented thalassophile who finds solace by drowning in the depths of poetry and spends his waking life painting, reading, writing, and engaging in conversations over black tea.

www.ingramcontent.com/pod-product-compliance
Lightning Source LLC
LaVergne TN
LVHW041642070526
838199LV00053B/3506